The New
Eighteenth-Century
Style

The New Eighteenth-Century Style

Rediscovering a French Décor

By MICHÈLE LALANDE

Photographs by GILLES TRILLARD

Conception and production by CORRINE PAUVERT THIOUNN

Translated from the French by LAUREL HIRSCH

ABRAMS, NEW YORK

Table of Contents

Preface

For some, the eighteenth century and the Age of Enlightenment remain defined by the extraordinary philosophical ideologies that brought an end to a thousand years of monarchial rule and ushered in the French Revolution. The death of Louis XIV and the rise of Napoléon Bonaparte are separated by a mere three-quarters of a century, a period marked by the long reign of Louis XV. When he dared, Louis XV was an artistic and inspired monarch whose court embodied an enduring model of taste and an artistic realm borne by an unprecedented momentum. While the monarchy was haplessly dying, he took his quest for elegance, refinement, and beautiful objects to new heights.

In royal residences such as Versailles, Parisian town houses, aristocratic estates, and the châteaux of the nouveaux riches, artists and artisans alike found their talents in demand by a discerning and privileged clientele. In the courts of Louis XV and Louis XVI, as in high society, it was obligatory to maintain one's station by exhibiting wealth and lineage through pomp and circumstance.

With a nod to the Age of Enlightenment and nostalgia for a lifestyle that has never truly vanished, the homes presented in this book all exude the heady scent of the eighteenth century. Far from museumlike reproductions or opulent décors bearing the signature of some grand master, these settings suffice with just a few pieces of furniture, some random objects, or a carefully placed painting, and the distinct manner in which they are laid out. Also shown in this volume is a reinterpretation of eighteenth-century style as it appeared in Sweden during the reign of Gustav III—a period of severe economic trouble that nonetheless saw a revival of the grandeur of French Enlightenment homes, albeit in much more modest versions and with the use of local materials.

Gustavian art favored a simple approach to furnishings, incorporating colors that have softened with the passage of time, as well as fabrics marked by a sense of sobriety. It is a faded eighteenth century—as if haloed in the powder used on wigs during that era—a time when tastes, all the same, tended toward vibrant, sometimes even violent colors; an eighteenth century of country houses, minor nobility, and a provincial middle class rid of all its gilding and ostentation.

The magic of this decorating craze lies in its adaptability to one's own taste and how readily nineteenth- and twentieth-century furniture and objects can be joined together into an intimate puzzle composed of odd pieces found here and there, abandoned during the turmoil of the Revolution, dispersed and forgotten over the centuries. Worn pieces of woodwork, a picket candlestick used as a lamp stand, a period stuffed chair, an old restored piece of furniture—all coalesce in a secret alchemy, a new harmony, the perfection of an opus that seems to have rediscovered the golden rule.

In this reconceived eighteenth century, even curio cabinets do not compare to these extraordinary collections of rare and unique objects from unknown worlds. Presented as the basis of a décor, albeit an undoubtedly unusual one, the curios are arranged in such a way as to become everyday objects. Today's smaller interior spaces make it impossible to exhibit these singular objects, to say nothing of the enormous bookcases that once held thousands of volumes. But don't a few antique books, rebound in leather and placed atop a chest of drawers, suffice to awaken the imagination?

In the pages of this beautiful book, through the interiors—all different, but each with a shared soul—Michèle Lalande and Gilles Trillard invite us on a journey into a prestigious past blended into the present. For our distinct pleasure, they have, with great talent, opened the door to the new eighteenth century.

&ppp; Annie-Camille Kuentzmann

A Curio Cabinet

Left: A set of Medici vases rhythmically adorns the staircase, creating, step-by-step, a sculptural impression.

Top right: Atop a greenhouse table, Neptune in all his grandeur watches over this Louis XV sofa that sits beneath the remains of an antelope massacre. Several framed specimens of beetles are also displayed.

Bottom right: This small, plain, repatinated sideboard, with its black painted top, serves as a sublime altar for Saint Elizabeth. Accented by picket candlesticks, it is guarded by a pair of seagulls. Rusted keys are displayed in two small wall showcases.

It was a strange journey that Christophe Hervé, a student of micromechanics, and Emmanuel San Martino, a student at the School of Fine Arts in Aix-en-Provence, embarked upon, becoming virtuosi of hairstyling and makeup, hopping from plane to plane, from Paris to New York, passing through London and Rome, to make up the stars.

One has held onto his brushes, the other has turned in his scissors to follow the scent of a flower. Today, they cultivate their shared passion for the rose: secretly discovering one at some horticulturist that had been handpicked somewhere in France, hunting for one before dawn as if it were an antique, partaking in the birth of a new variety. To attract them, a rose must have a certain *esprit*—it must be unique, expressive, vibrant, evolutionary, and rich in character.

In their amazing Paris shop Odorantes, their talent as floral decorators comes forward in an atmosphere of undergrowth, beneath the shade of gray walls the color of rain-washed zinc. Here, a profusion of exceptional roses are displayed in black Medici vases. Recently, antique objects like couches, lamps, and garden furniture have been mixed in with the flowers, as their other passion is most definitely secondhand markets. With a penchant for eighteenth-century style, they have applied their prodigious talents to their apartment in the Halles neighborhood of central Paris, creating a fairy-tale atmosphere where Sleeping Beauty and Prince Charming would feel right at home.

"This is, without question," they say in utter agreement, "the one place in the world where we feel best, because each piece of furniture, each object hunted down with love, resonates a little like a childhood memory."

Initially, the only interesting aspects of this apartment were the simple wooden ladders that accessed the old bedrooms in the garret and the exposed stone walls. With impeccable talent and taste, they transformed these rather bland rooms into an eccentric space of romance and harmony that invites the visitor to travel into a dreamworld.

Their talents as event designers are sought by everyone who's anyone in Paris. Each gala bears their signature—"flesh-colored" garden roses, fragrant roses and orchids, red and black roses, roses and ivory grapes—themes that serve as pretexts for their intimate and personalized compositions. Jean-Paul Gauthier, Givenchy, Céline, Rochas, Chanel, Jean Patou, and many others have become ardent devotees of their celebrated rose arrangements: people on the trail of a scent. ❧

Left: The kitchen is separated from the sitting room by a curtain of dyed boxwood beads. A section of a frieze, the kind found on a pergola, adorns the doorway. An oak pedestal table, its surface painted black and waxed, stands beneath a nineteenth-century garden lantern and in front of the wooden shutters.

Right: A mythological plaster bust, a gray-blue piece of coral, and a bouquet of pigeon feathers set in a jardiniere form a splendid still life.

Left: From their
numerous journeys
through Africa, the
owners developed
a fascination with
the wild fauna of the
savannah and great
lakes. They purchased
a taxidermist's
entire collection
and thereafter have
lived in the company
of a crowned crane,
a rhea, a white
spoonbill, cockatoos,
a Bassan gannet,
a puffin, Indian
pigeons, an eagle, a
goldfinch, a bird-of-
paradise, an African
bee-eater, and a
seagull.

Right: On a table
sit a truer-than-life
swan, the skull of a
warthog, a framed
longicorn, and
several masks from
Tanzania, Kenya,
and the Nubia region.

Left: A beautiful lesson in style, this palette of colors blends delightfully with a variety of grays—pearl, turtledove, stormy, as well as the pinkish and bluish grays of the dried hydrangea, the matte gray of the zinc and wrought iron, and the gray of the waxed and patinated furniture— all shades popular during the Age of Enlightenment.

Right: A Medici vase with Black Wanda orchids sits atop a nineteenth-century garden table in the company of a crown from a production of the operetta *King Lear.* Between the two windows, beneath an anatomical depiction, a wooden balustrade is used as a table.

A Poetry Lesson

$\mathcal{T}$his is the story of an exclusive and obsessive passion that nonetheless is utterly reasonable and controlled for the style of the Age of Enlightenment. It is the story of Florence, who could not imagine living without any one of these pieces of furniture and objects chosen with such discrimination that have become an integral part of her life. Current trends are not in force here, as perpetuity holds the reins. The ensemble is so coherent and harmonious, each object so well researched, that it seems to have been born in this very apartment in the Latin Quarter of Paris during the nineteenth century.

The apartment, with its red hexagonal tile and parquet floors, tall windows that still have their casements, woodwork festooned with moldings, and towering ceiling, was ideally suited to the décor. During the past century, several additional

Preceding page:
A stereoscope that dates from 1850, an apothecary scale, and an eighteenth-century sculpted wooden lamp are displayed atop an imposing Louis XVI–period chest. The portraits, most likely of Scandinavians, are from the same period.

Left: The Regency-period walnut crossbow chest of drawers displays an articulated wooden horse that was used as a model in an artist's studio.

Right: Beneath a restored spiral staircase stands a lone wooden horse taken from his herd.

rooms were added on the story below and made accessible by a spiral staircase found at a salvager's shop.

Initially, a few pieces of furniture from the family set the tone, but the mistress of the house then relinquished herself to the joys of antique-hunting; ever since, she has worked to complete and perfect the interior. Each object is not merely singular, but also recounts a story, an anecdote from a bygone era. Pure refinement. ❧

Right: A Boisselot-signed piano accentuates this lavish wainscoting. The *vanitas* above the mantelpiece, evoking death, dates from the seventeenth century.

Right: *Déjeuner sous les ombrages* (*Lunch in the Shadows*) is an anonymous painting from the eighteenth century. Placed next to the small Provençal desk of the same period is a Louis XV chair that still has its original upholstery.

Left: The alcoves of this room have been transformed into bookcases. Two doors have been removed and shelves now display all sorts of objects: masterworks, *santons* from Provence, gilded wooden angels, and watercolors.

Right: A wood and leather model sits atop this mantelpiece, along with a papier-mâché toy horse.

Fart left:
The Directoire bed
is complemented
by a mirror draped
like a bed canopy
in a Jouy cloth.

Top: A shelf sports a
hand-cranked acrobat
and a pair of
modeling hands.

Left: A cocked metal
hat that had been
used as a shop sign
adorns the *fronton*
of an alcove.

A Retrieved Memory of a Normandy Château

Left: In this mansion imprinted by the past, each piece of furniture, each placed object is an integral part of the home's history. The wooden urn, sculpted in the form of a draped cloth aflame (likely a church ornament) is placed on an elegant stone mantelpiece that dates from the construction of the building. The original mirror has been replaced with a more recent one, but the placement of the original pier can still be seen.

Nestled along the border between Normandy and Brittany, this 1726 manor house is known to the villagers as "Le Château." Impressive, albeit a bit austere, the main granite building is flanked by two symmetrical wings and sports a pretty, finely worked gate.

During the French Revolution, the château had almost been reduced to ashes, but fortunately, the village priest made sure the *sans-culottes* only set fire to the furniture and any object with the image of Louis XVI.

During the past centuries, the building had been inhabited by the landlords' farmers, who only

Top left: A convent table (with pigeon-holes for the nuns' napkins), surrounded by six eighteenth-century solid oak Dutch chairs, is posed on a floor of seventeenth-century granite slabs from the region. To replicate the color of patinated zinc, the tabletop has been recovered with oxidized iron leaf.

Center left: A set of frames and wooden pique candlesticks sit atop a cabinet originally from a bookshop.

Bottom left: Against a wall near the kitchen door, the owner has created an original composition atop an old grain chest. Next to a portrait of an "Aunt Jeanne," on wrapping found in the attic that must be as old as Methuselah, the owner has clipped a letter written by his predecessors, in an ink that has faded with time. Protected by wedding globes, two figures from a Neapolitan crèche sit on the head of an angel, which is itself attached to a piece of paneling.

occupied the main room on the ground floor. To facilitate the maintenance, the tile floors disappeared beneath a layer of cement, and later linoleum was used to cover beautiful oak parquet. The other rooms on both sides, along with those on the second floor, were used as a warehouse—a usage that, if nothing else, preserved the memories of the house.

Dutch by birth and the son of an antiques dealer, Peter Gabriëlse worked as a theater and television director in Amsterdam and Hilversum when he was not decorating stalls for antiques fairs in Brussels and Maastricht. When the time came for him to retire, he was enraptured by the lure of theatrical designs—so much so that he took to recreating them using old materials, in miniature three-dimensional forms that he set within a showcase. These works, as romantic as they are nostalgic, have seen great success, particularly in the United States.

A confirmed bachelor who jealously protects his solitude, Gabriëlse searched for an old house, preferably a dusty one with a history. When he bought this beautiful eighteenth-century residence, he sensed that his life would be turned upside down; here was a setting with such a rich past, filled with so many mysteries. As the new master of the estate, these secrets became clear to him with the passage of time.

Rising at dawn, retiring as night falls, with just a short break for a quick and frugal lunch, he searches for traces of the original history of his house. With the occasional help of a friend or a neighbor for the heaviest work, he has knocked down the plaster soffits and false ceilings, stripped the floors, and patiently removed layers of wallpaper, rediscovering the colors and patinas of times past. From this endless endeavor, he derives infinite pleasure.

Today, it is difficult to tell the difference between the restored rooms and those that remain in their original state, as they all seem to have passed through the centuries with the same serenity and endurance. During the course of this long project, he has made a few gratifying discoveries, such as the red hexagonal floor tiles (*tomettes*) and the superb oak parquet, the beams under the false ceiling, and, in the attic, an altar adorned with a Maltese cross. This last discovery moved him to create a kind of small chapel in the garret. Finally, carved into the steps of the granite staircase, he found three small circles that likely were put there to ward off bad luck and banish evil spirits. ❧

Right: Even missing its pier glass, this mirror has the charm of an object that has weathered the passage of time. The twisted column has been salvaged from a long-gone baldachin. The small rustic cabinet was part of a set from a bookshop; a matching one is found in the adjoining boudoir. The carrack, a blue faience named for the Portuguese ships generally used to import such pieces from China during the seventeenth century, dates from the Wan Li period. The small figurines are funerary statuettes that adorned graves in China.

Top left: This staircase was restored to its original green patina, which had been hidden beneath many coats of finish. The stone goddess, a mythological figure, was a fireplace pillar.

Bottom left: A few steps higher up, a sculpture of the Virgin Mary from the Middle Ages, which survived the throes of the French Revolution, is displayed near a superb stone holy-water basin.

Bottom center and right: A perfect reproduction of a *portego* bench from a Tuscan palace was constructed from old salvaged wood, as were a pair of stands on which sit two sculpted wooden church urns.

Right: The bedroom partition was stripped and a decorative panel with a pastoral motif, recovered from another room in the château, has been hung like a painting on the raw wood. A model of a boat, produced by a connoisseur, sits on the rustic table.

Left: The soft gray
patina of the hallway
leads to a bedroom
alcove. The stand is
covered in lead leaf
in the same manner
as the dining table.
The two eighteenth-
century Dutch
pastels, the hanger
with the linen shirt,
and the seatless chair
(on display merely
for its faded colors)
bestow a theatrical
feel upon the setting.

Above: In the
bedroom, where the
wallpaper is over a
hundred years old,
the contemporary
Dutch bed is a fine
complement to the
Louis XVI sofa. The
painting above the
bed, which was found
in the attic, has been
returned to its
rightful place.

Preceding pages:
In another building a few steps from the main house is the owner's secret spot—a place reserved for dreaming. With the countryside as a tranquil backdrop,

and within the warmth of timber several centuries old, are a painted wooden Normandy chest of drawers, a long rustic table, finials, and a bed frame fitted with an old mattress.

Left and above:
The ambience of this studio seems unreal and odd. Nevertheless, it brims with activity. With his panoply of old tools hunted down at garage sales, the artist works on his

sculptures—replicas of stage sets in miniature that he makes from old wood. In the small but stunning library, he has arranged more than a hundred tiny books, all rebound in

leather. Each element of the set décor—for example, the old windows and the clockmaker's ladder—is meticulously made by hand with great attention to detail.

In Praise of the Lovely Anjou

Left: In this seventeenth-century country house, all the rooms on the ground floor have double exposure. Throughout the day, light floods in through the large French doors that open onto the garden. Most of the furniture comes from an antiques shop very near the house.

Very close to Angers, deep in the Mauges region, there remains a small sunken lane cutting through the fields (a real Chouan path) that discretely leads to a farm and two forgotten country houses.

During the eighteenth century, these residences belonged to the Poulain de Cintré family, Angers aristocrats who divided their time between their town house in the old quarter of Angers and these pretty houses in Tranchandières. They experienced the dark hours of the Reign of Terror, when organized bands of brigands, passing as Chouans on the run, forced open the doors of the châteaux and first killed off the inhabitants, then plundered the places. Such was the fate of Madame de Cintré, a widow who lived alone in this mansion. On the sad night of 26 Prairial Year II (June 14, 1794), she was thrown onto the fire in her hearth and her house was completely ransacked.

Above: The black-and-white checkerboard floor pattern dates from the time of construction and covers a large part of the house, creating a beautiful unity of space.

Left: The harmony of the pearl-gray tones in the natural wood, the choice of whitewash, and the furniture creates a gentle serenity.

Top right: To maximize the effect of the light in the sitting room and the dining room, the doors between the two have been removed. The bookcase was purchased with the house; its patina was done in the old style and doors were added to the lower section. Family portraits are displayed among objects found at secondhand shops.

Left and bottom right: To replicate earlier times, the kitchen has been redone with a sink and work surface constructed and colored from a block, and then sanded. An artisan ironworker was hired to remake the window frames and door based upon the original design.

Of pre–Louis XIV construction, the buildings had been renovated through the centuries to become three long, low houses with double exposures that are very pleasant to live in. All the rooms open onto two sides of the garden amid trees that are several hundred years old. The roofs are fitted with a row of skylights typical of the Louis XIV era, giving the house a beautiful allure.

The mansion had recently been inhabited by an antiques dealer from Angers. One of her young clients, who passed the house every day on his way to law school, always had his eyes set on it and happily was able to buy it. He and his wife were deter-mined, as far as possible, to retain the soul of this beautiful place filled with such history.

They liked the mansion's quaint character, its dilapidated walls of peeling paint, and its feeling of an old house comfortable with its own character. Thus, they did only a minimal amount of work. The foyer, which at some point had been transformed into a kitchen, was returned to its original purpose. A new kitchen was installed at the far end of the building near the entry gate. Throughout, the walls were simply whitewashed and the ceiling beams were painted a pale blue-gray. ✂

Above: First and foremost, a gentleness is ever present in these rooms, with a tendency toward the exclusion of colors and preeminence given to light.

Above: The gray patina of the wooden shutters is set center stage, with the walls, accessories, and antique bed linens all in white. The sole figurative element in the bedroom is the natural linen drapery created by the painter Thérèse Jamin, using designs inspired by eighteenth-century chinoiserie.

The Carpenter's House

More than half of Sweden is covered with vast forests. When leaving Stockholm to pay a visit to Stephan and Paola Söder, one must follow a multitude of serpentine lanes that lace around the white trunks of birch trees.

All of a sudden, a green and hilly expanse dotted with wooden houses all painted the same red pops up. In the past, the paint was made from the copper-rich earth giving Swedish houses their unity of color. By adding flour and water, an ecological, economical, and reliable product was produced. This same recipe is used today to create this inimitable "Swedish" red and there are people who travel here just to buy it.

The Söders' house, which sits on a hilltop, is naturally also painted red, its doors and windows framed in white. Stephan, who is a cabinetmaker, a carpenter, and a painter, applies his many talents in his studio located in a small house a few steps away. There, he creates huge eighteenth-century-style painted panels.

Their house is simple and natural, with neither fanfare nor artificiality. Soft, discreet colors are used throughout the space, giving prominence to the surrounding countryside that enters through all the windows and doors. Except for those pieces passed down through the family, the couple found all the old furniture antique hunting throughout Sweden, highlighting their preference for folk art. ✜

Preceding page: A pure Swedish simplicity defines this house, built in 1702. The brilliance of the pine floor has been attained merely by using soap. The sobriety of the rustic eighteenth-century corner cupboard is in perfect harmony with the original hearth, which in earlier days was the main source of heat for the entire place.

Right: In past times, this black metal candlestick, with its fine silhouette, would have been placed in a niche of the hearth.

Right: The darkness of this granite floor is softened by the light blue-gray walls and the glossy patina of the old door. The surface of the half-moon table, overflowing with flowers and fruit from the garden, has been covered with a coat of zinc. Three rustic chairs designed for children stand in a row.

Far left: Distributed throughout the house, the Gustavian chairs, chests of drawers, and this desk have been painted either in gray or in this charming rust color (*right*) conventionally seen on rustic furniture.

Top left: A Gustavian-style painted panel, quite in vogue in Sweden, hangs in the studio.

Center left: The dining table, designed by the owner, was fashioned out of an old butcher's counter, replete with hack marks.

Bottom left: The brutal Swedish climate justifies a fireplace in each room of the house. All are made of plaster and are original to the house.

Right: Both the floors and ceilings are made of pine planks of variable dimensions.

Gently, Subtly Allying Styles

D espite the relentless tentacles of urbanization, there still remain a rare few old towns quite close to the center of Paris. Although the city is not far, these towns have managed to preserve the feel of a village from earlier times with protected streets, small shops, and reduced traffic—a gentler and more humane lifestyle.

It is in one of these towns, just west of Paris, that a designer and her historian husband chose to live—between Grande Rue, the Place de la Vierge, and Rue de Madame (named for the sister of the king). They were seduced by the setting of planted gardens with ancient trees and old houses in the middle of a district that has remained untouchable.

From the very start, the house exuded an undeniable charm, largely due to the expansion of the oldest section, which dates to the eighteenth century, undertaken at the beginning of the twentieth century. A new main building was then added, jutting out a little from the older buildings because of the slope of the land and providing rooms also a bit

Below: The Louis XV marble mantelpiece is adorned with a collection of plaster figurines bought at auction from a Paris studio.

Opposite top: The hallway between the present dining room and kitchen has been enlarged, and the wall separating them removed. The staircase has been redesigned with a banister that ends at a low wall, allowing the kitchen elements to come forward. During the demolition of the staircase, a

pretty wood and wrought-iron banister was discovered that now offers a new perspective to all the rooms it adjoins.

Opposite middle: The objects displayed on this eighteenth-century Swedish chest of drawers have been selected for their Venetian paint by the Orientalist Fernand Lantoine. The zinc lamp, fashioned out of a gutter funnel, is displayed with foliage candlesticks and a finial.

irregular—three steps here, four steps there—a rather lively and original interior architecture. Movement and brightness come naturally to this house, with its rooms on different levels and the light that streams through its many windows offering exposure in all directions.

For the décor, gentle and simple was the mode of choice. Even completely empty, this house was already very lovely. The mistress of the house is particularly fond of the plain, unpretentious Scandinavian style, and thus chose a scheme of paints in white, off-white, the lightest of yellows, and an even lighter gray—just a hint of color for the walls and a few shades deeper on the doors and beams. The old terra-cotta floors were then sanded, and the less interesting ones were covered over with rattan.

With spring coming, the garden has returned to life. Irises are sprouting, along with the primroses, the crocuses, and the forget-me-nots. These flowers are soon to be followed by wreaths of red roses climbing along the arches and bringing a shot of color to the house. ✌

Left: Three white-lacquered screens section off a corner of the sitting room. In front of an eighteenth-century stand are a garden statue and a wooden horse.

Preceding pages: A striped Swedish rug makes the sitting room appear larger. All the furnishings are contemporary— from the low table to the sofas upholstered in old monogrammed fabrics. The Gustavian clock comes from Sweden. On each side of the fireplace is a Louis XVI stuffed chair upholstered in an Aubusson tapestry depicting *The Fables* of La Fontaine.

Left: Shelves have been affixed to otherwise unadorned walls. The mirror of a repainted armoire set at an angle enlivens the room by dispersing light passing through the window.

Right: In the clarity of the afternoon, the color of the basketry blends with the golden tones of the oak Louis XVI chest of drawers and the nineteenth-century Venetian fan-shaped watercolor seascape.

In Angers, Benedictine Nuns for Neighbors

Preceding pages:
Inside, a multitude of
objects is assembled
as a still life: a clock,
pieces of zinc roofing,
oeils-de-boeuf,
finials, valences,
stacks of paper and
rebound books, hat
boxes, empty cartons,
and candlesticks.

Right and opposite:
A large window was
installed in a child's
bedroom to make the
most of the view onto
the garden-terrace.
The chest of drawers
is a contemporary
rendition of an
eighteenth-century
original. Two framed
leaf motifs are
displayed on an
easel next to the
nursing chair.

his is the strange story of a metamorphosis,
a radical change of destiny when a factory,
under the baton of a talented and intrepid decorator, became a family home.

During the last century, on one side of the street
there had been a shoe factory and across from it,
the imposing seventeenth-century Benedictine
convent. In the past, the two buildings were con-
nected underground, allowing the nuns to escape
in case of an emergency. Over the course of the
years, the shoe factory was replaced by a house-
painting studio. A daring and inspired antiques
dealer then bought the building and in record time
gave the place (which had not been suitable for
habitation) the warm ambience of a home.

Originally, the lower portion of the roof was
glass and the upper portion, slate. The usage of the
materials was reversed to make the most of the di-
rect view onto the stars.

On the ground floor, in what was sometimes a
sitting room, sometimes a warehouse, the cement
floor was retained and the space left unaltered.
Stunning objects have found their place here, like
an enormous clock from a train station that hangs
above a Chesterfield couch, a zinc finial, sculpted
wooden angels' wings, balusters, and an oeil-de-
boeuf window—a real hodgepodge of furniture and
objects that brings to mind the wings of a theater
where a grand opera is about to be staged rather
than the home of a decorator. All these arrangements of eighteenth- and nineteenth-century items
evince a sense of whimsy and a touch of humor, ev-
idence of a true talent at work.

An openwork staircase leads to the second floor. This is where, under the metal superstructure, between the steel girders and the white-painted cement walls, the mistress of the house has placed the living quarters. In this industrial setting, she has succeeded in creating an atmosphere filled with romance and harmony, bathed in light. Set on a parquet of broad, blond oak floorboards, here is a single visual expanse that is cleverly divided with glass partitions that give a view of the sitting area, terrace, and garden on one side and the Benedictine convent, whose bells provide a delectable rhythm to the day, on the other side. ❧

Herbier de E. BAUDOUIN

HERBIER DE E. Baudouin.

Herbier de E. BAUDOUIN

Preceding pages:
Along the upper level,
a series of windows
form a font of light
for the ground floor.
The garden-terrace
can be seen on
one side, while on
the other lies the
Benedictine convent.
A "flea-market" feel
pervades both inside
and out. On the lawn,
an array of bells,
mini-greenhouses,
birdcages, and
pottery are scattered
about randomly.

Left: Once again,
the "compilation"
works: an eighteenth-
century window
frame, sufficiently
faded; a garden
ornament; two
putti upending
an amphora; an
herbarium framed
in a window with
pretty, small square
moldings. This tiny
corner is further
enlivened by another
scene (*right*), this
one composed of
a pair of wooden
shutters serving as
partitions, an
artist's model,
and a painting—a
perspective over an
open attic, depicted
in a gentle harmony
of gray and white.

In the Palais Royal, a Little House under the Trees

Once associated with the beautiful town house next door, this small coachman's house has been given a new life. One could just imagine the clomping of the hooves as horses marched around in the square courtyard and drank from the stone fountain. Today, the street sounds are somewhat more prosaic, but the birds still come and nest in the trees above the planted flower beds.

Fabrice Diomard, an antiques decorator at the Village Suisse in Paris, is the happy resident. He has two passions—the eighteenth century and the "designer look." Specifically, Plexiglas. In pursuit of his ideas and talents, he set up two facing galleries displaying these two styles, which would seem difficult to combine. Nevertheless, he has been successful here in this little house near the Palais Royal.

He chose white, both to give a unity of color to the three rooms and to make them as bright as possible, as the sun's rays do not easily penetrate.

His collection of simple and transparent Plexiglas chairs and sofas leaves the limelight to the pieces of antique furniture that he has hunted down with meticulous care. The two masterpieces are, without question, the superb Gustavian bench and the stunning chest of drawers with its trompe l'oeil in gilded wood and mirrored marquetry that probably dates from the 1940s, inspired by eighteenth-century Venetian style. ❧

Preceding page:
This chest of drawers is a stunning and rare example of marquetry with glass and trompe-l'oeil drawers. (There are only eight drawers, although the chest appears to have sixteen.) Highlighted with gilded wood and inspired by eighteenth-century Italian style, it was discovered in Toulouse. A collection of antique plaster decorative motifs is displayed under Plexiglas.

Right: White and transparency are *de rigueur* for accentuating the Gustavian period banquette and its complementary Corbusier chaise longue. On the wall are works by Valérie Maffre and Jeanne Lacombe.

Left: This bedroom wall is decorated with framed pages from an herbarium. Next to it is a plaster statuette depicting a Greek athlete, bought at the same Paris studio auction as the statue in the sitting room. The chandelier is a creation of Fabrice Diomard.

Far right: A series of photographs by Karin Lhémon is displayed next to the shelves.

The Magic of Remembering

Left top and bottom:
Each room of this
apartment exhibits
a perfectly executed
scene set of furniture
and objects. An old
pediment provides
the chic aspect of a
bookcase, while the
more rustic structure
has simply been
whitewashed. A satin
Louis XVI shoe, the
Venetian lantern and
candlestick, and the
red chalk family
portrait are among
the mementos and
objects collected by
the mistress of the
home.

So as not to forget her much-loved earlier life in a large family house, Nicole Polonovski has brought to this more modest dwelling some of her furniture and all of its memories. She left behind grand rooms—with their tall casement windows framed by interior wooden shutters, their majestic double doors adorned with elaborate moldings, and their sweet-smelling waxed oak parquet floors. Yet with her magical talents, she has managed to bring back to life the setting of her past with love, romance, and elegance.

Located west of Paris, this small apartment initially possessed no particular charm and now overflows with it. The high-quality antique furniture, the Italian and Gustavian chests of drawers, the Louis XV stuffed chairs, the portraits of women from the eighteenth century, and the thousands of

objects and refined details have each found their perfect spots. This abundance, this accumulation of pretty things, has transformed the apartment into a charming and stunning universe.

In her spare time, the owner makes embroidered pillows, bedspreads, flowing drapes, and canopies from antique linens, all which serve to give her apartment a certain French chic. ❧

Right: The small lamps lit on December 8 during the Feast of the Immaculate Conception in Lyon are called "Lyonais."

Right: This sofa, for all its roundness, is a metal army cot adorned with soft, comfortable pillows. Sculpted wooden lamps sit atop wooden valises. Each corner is furnished with a nineteenth-century stela displaying a Medici vase. The wall-hanging is composed of a linen remnant on which an eighteenth-century gilded wooden pampre is centered.

Above left: Nothing could better complement the eighteenth-century oak chest than this stunning Italian Stations of the Cross from the same period.

Above right: The hallway is furnished with a piece from a boarding school and a Gustavian column on which a decorative garden fruit basket sits.

Above left: In front of
a nineteenth-century
pier, the dining
table, adorned with
a monogrammed
tablecloth, is
illuminated by
a Venetian lantern.
Two catacomb
lanterns are set before
the window.

Above right: The
linen-upholstered
sofa seems even
plumper because of
the zinc oeil-de-boeuf
hanging over it.

A House of Artists

In a hilly countryside where old, half-timbered farmhouses are set here and there, like the work of a naïf painter, this unique house catches the eye, a wink at its surroundings.

The passion of the artist does not go unnoticed. With salvaged old pieces of zinc, he constructs (solely for his own pleasure) pigeon coops, stunning chandeliers in the shapes of hot-air balloons and church bells. Kept outside because of their imposing size, these works surround the house in a halo of mystery. The artist also enjoys reproducing old signs and sculpting salvaged wood, with which he makes a variety of old-time baskets.

The architecture of this house, with its scalloptiled roof, is traditional of the Savoy region. At the beginning of the last century, the house sported two small verandas, one facing south, the other east. Unconventional for this style of residence, which dates to the mid-eighteenth century, the verandas did, however, add much charm to both the exterior and the interior, brimming as they did with green plants throughout the year. The wooden loggia on the second floor, which presently is enclosed in glass, confirms that we are in the Savoy. Now an attractive room, in previous times it was used for spreading and drying the animal fodder that would then be used in the winter.

Several years ago, the mistress of the house opened a secondhand shop a few miles away. She primarily hunts for eighteenth- and nineteenth-century country furniture and objects, with a preference for unusual, original pieces that possess a particular charm or *esprit*. Keen on popular art, her house most definitely reflects her shop. With two

staircases, three steps here, four steps there, and almost all the rooms on different levels, a varied décor is in order.

Painted regional furniture and sundry unexpected objects—clustered in abundance with an eye to setting the scene (not forgetting the humor and sense of whimsy)—give the house a unique and romantic atmosphere. ❧

Page 87: A collection of incomparable blue Saint-Omer faience pitchers.

Left: Beneath the strange gaze of two Baroque painted sheet-metal angels found in an abandoned chapel, the Louis XV bed is enhanced by this Aubusson tapestry.

Below left: Suspended from the roof of the winter garden, this hot-air balloon chandelier was made from salvaged pieces of zinc and sheet metal.

Left: The ogive window, also salvaged, was installed by the owners, as was the stone basin, found abandoned in the barn.

Above: The dining room is furnished with a long, rectangular patinated table. A Directoire soup tureen decorated with portraits of Henri IV and Marie-Antoinette sits atop a piece of jute. In earlier times, this bookcase, which still has its original copper color, had been an apothecary case.

Left: A biplane and
an angel fly above a
sitting area, adding
whimsy to a
comfortable room.

Above left: A
collection of
"Alpine memories"
hangs at the head
of the bed. These
pictures, made from
embroideries with
edelweiss motifs,
frame a photograph
of a soldier leaving
for war.

Above right: Greens
dominate this child's
bedroom. On the
patinated wooden
leaf-table sits a
marvelous cow on
wheels made from
old, heavy stockings.
On the wall hangs a
sort of silly lady made
from a pinecone in
the style of the folk
art found in the
Jura region.

93   *A House of Artists*

Left: The fireplace is draped in an antique Jouy cloth. A bronze candlestick is displayed near a processional figurine. On the small blue cabinet sit three brightly painted papier-mâché dolls, which in olden days were given to young mothers on the day they gave birth. A rare cherrywood violin case rests on the hearthstones.

Right: The roughness of the wall along the staircase has been preserved as a relic of the past. The walnut sculpture is the work of a wood sculpture studio. The painted metal of the Louis XV clock works perfectly with the dusky colored staircase.

Life in Verdigris

An avid collector of antiques now riding on the latest fashion of Gustavian furniture, Élisabeth Brac de la Perrière is considered one of the pioneers of painted furniture. She was among the first to open a shop—which quickly became an indispensable venue—selling eighteenth- and nineteenth-century furniture repatinated in the old style.

Her apartment is a reflection of her store and is almost as filled to overflowing with pieces of verdigris-colored furniture, thousands of objects crammed into dressers, Medici bowls filled with stocks of candlesticks, and zinc baskets stuffed with fragments of cornices, friezes, and other salvaged decorative bits and pieces. Shelves brim with Creil, Nevers, and Montereau faience, chests of drawers are packed with candelabras, and even the armoires cannot escape a collection of wickerwork and birdcages.

This collection, ever faithful to the unity of color, sets the tone and charm of the scene. The eye cannot refrain from scouring, examining, and feasting upon the array. Naturally, with all her discoveries and antique shopping, one item tumbles onto the next, and it is this perpetual movement, in both the apartment and in the shop, that seduces her friends as much as her guests. ✂

With its mishmash array of objects and arrangements of bric-a-brac, a flea-market feel permeates this house. Despite appearances, it is a well-ordered universe—a place where you feel comfortable, with the atmosphere similar to an antiques shop.

Above left: Like most of the furnishings, this Louis XV table, with a verdigris finish, is set amid an apparent disarray of eighteenth-century chairs and stuffed chairs. The tabletop in front of the window brims with zinc roof finials, some of which have been made into lamps.

Above center: The Louis XVI–period breakfront is filled with eighteenth-century Creil, Digoin, and Lunéville faience. On the upper shelf is an elegant Nevers soup tureen.

Above right: The abundance of objects in the sleeping quarters accentuates its intimacy. Leaning against the wall at the head of the bed is an eighteenth-century pastel portrait of a young boy, and behind the Louis X pedestal table are a Medici vase and a painted wooden barometer. The window drapes are made of linen. The mauve-colored eighteenth- and nineteenth-century Provençal bedding is particularly refined.

Right: On the unusual Eastern European desk sit gilded glass candlesticks and three antique vodka glasses—stemless, so once emptied, they could be carried on one's shoulders.

The Eighteenth Century in Black and White

$\mathcal{A}$ couturier by profession and the creator of collections in which femininity and subtlety come together, Marcel Marongiu has a fondness for soft colors—from sky gray to sea foam—that flow with elegance and lend an exceptional refinement to the supple textures of his dresses.

Emblematic of his eclectic nature, Marongiu has taken a completely different approach with his Paris apartment, located midway between the Opéra and the column in Place Vendôme, which he can admire at leisure from his terrace on the top floor of his nineteenth-century building.

The son of a French father and a Swedish mother, he spent the first ten years of his life in Sweden. From the northern lights and his family house, filled with Gustavian furniture, to the paintings faded with the passage of time, he has held onto a certain nostalgia.

A young man on the go and a great traveler under the spell of India, his aesthetic choices bear the imprint of his discoveries. He has conceived his home as a reflection of himself, bringing together a Rajasthani armoire and a Fragonard engraving.

While his studio is in a constant state of creative flux, he has chosen a balance between the contemporary and the classic for his apartment—eighteenth- and nineteenth-century works mingle with contemporary furniture. There is no color present to trouble the waters. Only black and white is to be seen amid the verdigris of the sofas and stuffed chairs. ✂

Page 103: Two eighteenth-century balusters displayed on a pair of metal stacking tables designed by the owner of the house.

Opposite top: A Louis XV stuffed chair upholstered in white and a white-covered sofa are offset by two naturally faded screens and low Indian tables repainted in black.

Bottom left and right: Collections include Medici vases and Gustavian candlesticks, some antique, others reproductions.

Following pages: An eighteenth-century Flemish painting depicting the Holy Family hangs in the bedroom along with a fine collection of etchings by Fragonard, Le Brun, Le Corrège, and Poussin—in a word, an eclectic décor conceived by an artist in love with mystery and the unforeseen.

In the Heart of Paris, an Atelier Revisited

*I*n the back of a Paris courtyard, behind a glass façade, there was a man who repaired typewriters. But with the advent of new technology, the day came when he had to hang up his wares, as it was just too expensive to modernize. The atelier closed its pretty glass doors and remained dormant for a good ten years. Despite its antiquated state, filled as it was with machines, Laure du Chatenet and her husband nonetheless decided to buy it. "We hadn't even seen the beams. The walls were completely hidden behind overflowing shelves, but we immediately liked the space and decided on the spot."

There was no running water or electricity, and after some extensive clearing out, work began on the recreation of an old house. They retained the sixteen-foot (five-meter) height above the dining room where the superstructure served as the ceiling. A mezzanine was built halfway up, covering two-thirds of the surface to create a second floor for the bedrooms and bathrooms. These new rooms are accessed by a ramp bordered with an antique wooden handrail.

Passionate about antiques, Laure du Chatenet, along with her childhood friend Gwenaëlle Roché, opened a shop right near the Arc de Triomphe. La Maison Caumont is housed in the old stables of a Haussmann building with each stall presenting a different eighteenth-century décor, assiduously reproduced by these talented antiques decorators. They will soon be launching a collection of original furniture and objects inspired by the eighteenth century, which will be handcrafted according to the old techniques and which will feature non-treated woods. ❧

Opposite top: Suspended from a wood beam, this grand chandelier came from a château in western France.

Opposite bottom right: A thick slab of oak transforms a metal factory counter into a dresser. Breaking with the more academic ambience created by the library elements, it a gives a certain character to the room.

Above left: Behind the spiral staircase stands a multicolored wooden statue of Saint Margaret, found in central France.

In the bedroom is an
eighteenth-century
cherrywood chest
of drawers. The style
has been dubbed
"Parisian" because it
was intended for the
small rooms located
just under the roofs.
A pair of lamps made
from pieces of
sculpted wood from
the same period
accessorize the room.

The walls of the
sitting room are
accented with wood
panels that serve as
a pretty background
for an elegant
eighteenth-century
mirror. A low table
has been made from
salvaged slab of wood
flooring set on a
metal structure.

Outrelaise: Romance and Tradition

An old French saying goes, "Qui veut se tenir à son aise, ne doit point sortir outrelaize." ("He who longs to ease his days, need go no farther than the banks of the Laize.") Etched into the 1614 black marble plaque at the entry of the château, these lines were a warm welcome to the passing guest, and a fine omen. In fact, Jean-Louis Mennesson and Walid Akkad, the new masters of this historic estate, have made hospitality their preferred pastime.

Constructed during the sixteenth century, the imposing edifice that stands today bears little semblance to the original building. Over the centuries it has been witness to historical events and home to eminent landlords, including an advisor to Henri IV who bought it in 1569. He enlarged and restored the several facing outbuildings in order to have a place to escape the hubbub of the royal court. Upon his death, his nephew took over the estate, which then passed to the hands of the Marquise de Chambors, a young widow whose husband, a squire of Louis XV, had been fatally wounded during a hunt with hounds organized by the king's son. During her long years of solitude, the marquise brought the tastes of the day to the château, added a low wing, and created a large garden by removing two-thirds of the outbuildings. Inside, the grand staircase was reconstructed, preserving the magnificent wrought-iron banister signed "Roche M. F." and dated 1780.

The marquise's granddaughter, the Countess de Polignac, hired the renowned Chatelain brothers to redesign the hilly land through which the Laize River and its tributaries flow. This exalted past convinced the current landlords to restore the interiors in keeping with their own taste, but always remaining mindful of history. While completely preserving the interior architecture, they brought life and light back to the ground floor by painting the walls light tones. The bedrooms on the second floor exhibit bolder harmonies that were chosen after several color tests.

The entire estate—the château, grounds, vegetable garden, and flower garden—are continually evolving. Today, Outrelaise is the ideal setting for organized events, festivals, meetings, and seminars. Its spaces, like the variety of its décor, lend themselves to photography shoots and film sets, assuring—with new actors and new encounters—the continuance of this site imbued with history. ❧

Right: The play of perspectives underscores the elegance of this château's majestic entryway and accentuates the Louis XVI–period wrought-iron banister by Roche. A collection of eighteenth- and nineteenth-century lanterns sits on a console of the same period. Two processional lanterns are displayed on the landing.

Above left: The dining table, simply covered in a linen sheet, stands beneath a theater chandelier. An eighteenth- century decorative panel on cloth hangs above the monastic fireplace.

Above right: The pantry is filled with homemade jams and preserves made from produce grown in the garden.

Right: To preserve truffles, the glass jars must be thick-walled and tinted dark.

Above: The size
of this kitchen is
impressive. The
Normandy farm
table is set on
a floor of Caen
stone slabs.

Above left:
A collection of glass
carafes is displayed on
a shelf over the bright
blue stove.

Above right:
The same painted
paneling decorates
the pantry, which
often is used as
a storage room.
The tall chair is
a cashier's seat.

Following pages:
The tall windows
of the sitting room,
with their interior
shutters, oak parquet
floor, and festooned
wainscoting and
moldings, comprise

the décor of
this magnificent
room. The Louis XV
chairs are simply
upholstered in white.
The daybed and its
pillows provide a glint
of color.

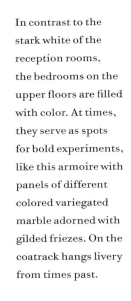

In contrast to the stark white of the reception rooms, the bedrooms on the upper floors are filled with color. At times, they serve as spots for bold experiments, like this armoire with panels of different colored variegated marble adorned with gilded friezes. On the coatrack hangs livery from times past.

The Ephemeral as a Way of Life

*H*er house, on the edge of the village, seems to have come straight from a postcard praising the wonders of Normandy. Provençal by birth and in her heart, Annie-Camille, who adores change, had found her old place too small.

She decided to look for a home in the region of La Beauce, as it is both close to Paris and pure countryside: a true change of scenery, far from the noise and pollution of the big city.

As soon as she entered the sitting room, with its cathedral structure and tall windows looking out directly onto the fields, she immediately understood that it would be the ideal context to satisfy her wild passion for the Enlightenment, an obsession she tirelessly developed through books found hidden away in secondhand shops. She has always rummaged, transformed, replaced, and incessantly changed the placement of things, not in search of perfection, but merely to acquiesce her desire for change.

Her first concern was to find the best color balance to lighten the rooms and to radiate the soft ambiance in which she felt so comfortable displaying furniture and objects. Her house beats to the rhythm her heart finds. With her indefatigable pleasure for arranging, she is continually on the lookout for objects that will inspire an idea for a new setting in her home. Once completed, these still lifes have a very short life span, as they are quickly supplanted by new arrangements. Here, furniture never stands still.

The dining room, with its vaulted ceilings and whitewashed beams, is the soul of the house. On the loftlike mezzanine, she has made a guestroom worthy of Sleeping Beauty.

On the ground floor, the hallway to the kitchen is partially blocked by a dresser, the back of which is hidden behind a screen fashioned out of old wooden shutters. From the bedroom, with its two

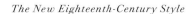

Left: Beneath a splendid eighteenth-century gilded wooden chandelier stands a small oak and fruitwood table.

Above: This zinc pigeon atop his perch, shot full of holes by hunters, was once a finial ornament.

Right: A lamp, fashioned from some bases and a column, stands between a repatinated apothecary case. a small notary's desk piled with hbooks.

In past times, curio cabinets were filled with rare and unusual objects brought back from far-off places. Today, they are more romantic and, whether through affinity or a harmony of colors, assemble objects marked by the passage of time.

large glass doors that open directly onto the garden, one could imagine one was sleeping in the nearby flowerbeds.

Her ideas for the garden are also quite creative. She collects all sorts of old cages, which hang from walls wildly covered with ivy, arrays of watering cans, and terra-cotta pots skillfully stacked. Small pedestal tables rusted by the rain and overflowing with salvaged zinc objects have been brought back to life by her talented and inspired hands. She knows how to take part of a small, abandoned greenhouse or some forgotten arbor and transform it into a delightful altar on which she places three or four unusual objects.

This woman of many talents gives free rein to her creativity and emotions, all to make her house an enchanted spot overflowing with sweetness and romance. ❧

Following pages:
In this space reserved for inspiration, the furniture and objects lie in wait before taking the place of other pieces that, for the moment, remain in the house. But this storage spot, which looks like the wings of a theater, is as keenly arranged as if it were a huge curio cabinet.

Above left and right: In the kitchen, even the smallest details have been carefully addressed—the gilded bronze pendant chandelier, the Directoire larder, the small nineteenth-century tables, the zinc finial.

Above: Among the functional items are linen dishcloths stacked behind earthenware dishes from Saint-Omer, Saint-Clément and Apt, marble fruit, a set of eighteenth-century Chantilly plates, and an enamel pitcher for garden flowers.

Left: An homage to beautiful objects: A clutch of votive candles lie on a linen cloth in a Medici vase. Here and there are placed an array of objects, such as a Wedgwood terrine and, in front of a metal tray painted with the Agen coat-of-arms, a covered bowl made of fine faience.

Right: With its hunting trophies, its simple bouquets of branches stuck in a pair of Medici vases, the company of some ducks and a partridge, and a bedspread in ticking, the bedroom seems the perfect spot for Sleeping Beauty.

An American Passion

This is a medieval house, just next to the church, in a tiny Anjou village that is proud of its two main streets. Here, tradition has been maintained: Every weekday morning, at precisely seven o'clock, the church bell chimes thirty times to remind the few residents that the hour has come to go to the fields. This proved an irresistible echo of the past for Americans Stephen Shubel and Woody Biggs, one an interior architect and designer who applied his talents both in France and California, the other an antiques dealer who hunted throughout all of Europe for his West Coast clients. Based in San Francisco, they have found a second life in this village, one that is more authentic and moves to a completely different rhythm than a large American city.

They have used the three stories of this sixteenth-century house to create three open spaces, each with its own purpose. The ground floor is used as a sitting room/dining room; the second floor is entirely devoted to a bedroom/sitting area and sports a terrace that overlooks the garden; and in the converted attic, there is another bedroom and a studio area.

White reigns supreme on the walls highlighting their collections, and it is the objects and paintings, along with the ever-present nature, that bring color to the home. The evening light streams in through the new French doors that open onto the garden. But one of the charms of this five-hundred-year-old house is the mystery that emanates from its cellar.

It is accessed by a flat door set in the tile floor. Passing through, one discovers blocked passageways that once led to the church and the convent on the other side, as the house was once an annex. ❧

Page 139:
The impressive oak structure is the room's sole decoration. The beams embedded into the plaster serve as a large bookcase that covers one wall. The niches hold an array of objects, wickerwork and pottery, busts and trophies, all of which have found a new life in this setting.

Left: The mild climate of Anjou makes for a vibrant countryside— wisteria, mock orange, ferns, and ivy intermingle, creating a verdant backdrop beyond the French doors.

Right: The upper part of the niche in the entryway is closed off by doors that have been salvaged, making a small showcase near the eighteenth-century sculpted column, an elegant plinth for a fossil.

Left: Placed in front of the oak Regency mirror, a rustic table serves as a console. The double door in the rear formerly gave access to an underground passage that led to the church and the convent.

Right: The bedroom has been designed as a sitting room. The wide showcase, originally from an herbalist's shop, is filled with collected objects: a clock dial, church vases, sconces, apothecary jars, plaster busts, wickerwork, silver pieces, patinated bound books, and antique frames.

The Art of Composition

This is a farmhouse that does not follow the norm. The architect who designed this home in the early twentieth century—in the Brie region of France not far from Paris—added a touch of fun with the gables, canopies, and recesses, bringing a uniqueness that blends the charm of a family home with the advantages of expansive outbuildings.

If a house, however subtly, recounts the lives of its inhabitants, here is one that reveals the passions of Cléo Burtin in images that are both beautiful and simple. She has not only combed through flea markets, but through salvagers as well, replenishing her stock of sometimes odd and disconcerting objects. The outcome? An *arte povera:* an unexpected composition that verges on the luxurious but is always refined.

In each room of the house she abandons herself to her preferred pastime—bestowing a perfectly harmonious coexistence upon an array of apparently unrelated objects that come from far and wide. Emphasizing a gentle range of whites and excluding colors, she teases out the essence of objects, their *esprit* and resonance, and sets them center stage. It is as if they and Cléo Burtin were in cahoots, and those ties linking them serve as a source of inspiration. As soon as one crosses the threshold, a strange charm takes over, coercing the visitor to seek the thread that connects all these beautiful ideas in hope of appreciating them that much more.

The same creative spirit permeates the garden. Boxwood balls and market gardeners' bells are clustered among zinc items, old rusted gates, and miscellaneous garden elements she has picked up here and there. Having long reserved her finds for the privileged few, Burtin has found an original spot just east of the capital to present them to the public. ✍

Left: Methodically arranged on the bookshelves, which have been painted a discreet gray, is a collection of decoration magazines. The back of the Louis XVI sofa will not be restored, as its color is inimitable.

Right: Displayed on a black marble-top butcher's table is a collection of silver, with a plaster pediment from a door behind it. Beneath the chromos is a pair of sconces—a chandelier cut in two. Hanging from the ceiling is a Dutch pewter chandelier painted gray with small black-and-white lampshades.

Above right: Shelving from a studio, with rusted supports, has been transformed into a curio cabinet replete with pieces of cornices and balusters, plaster casts, lanterns, garden bells, stacks of books with broken bindings, and even an inspection lamp to illuminate everything.

Set before a stunning
piece of plaster
molding—originally
from paneling in
a château—is the
grace of a dove,
the transparency of
crystal carafes, and
the sheen of silver
bells (salvaged from
a chandelier that
has seen its day), all
placed atop a mirror.

Difficult to find in good condition, these tall and slender wooden shutters screen off the closet area of the bathroom, which has ten-foot (three-meter) ceilings. The bathtub, with its classic lion's-claw feet, repainted a vanilla yellow with white feet, stands before a white cotton drape.

Above left: An odd Directoire table, with it legs posed in an "X" and its worn surface, serves as a stage for a still life composed of a plaster fawn, a papier-mâché sheep's head, a wooden bear transformed into a candle-carrier, antiquarian books, and a flock of stuffed birds—robins, sparrows, and starlings. A pair of wings hangs next to the chandelier.

Above right: The lower part of the bedroom could have been paneled with the plaster that frames mirrors in Haussmann apartments. The bed, the meridienne sofa, and the chairs have been recovered with simple white cotton material.

Above: A collection of
restaurant silverware
found at secondhand
shops is displayed on
a butcher's table.

The Barn Deep in the Woods

nce upon a time, deep in the forest of Sologne, there was a huge abandoned barn. Well proportioned, with its brick and timber façade and its roof of old, locally made tiles sprouting moss, the barn cut a fine figure in the middle of a clearing between the ancient oak and linden trees. Only wild boar and deer found refuge there, far from hunters' shotguns.

This peaceful haven is where a designer and his family have chosen to make home. In the beginning, there were merely four walls and a roof. The family was set on keeping the wonderful height of the structure for the living room and the kitchen/dining area, so they split it in half to create an entryway and a second floor for the bedrooms. But to accommodate this large family, four more rooms were needed. An outbuilding next to the barn that had previously housed a chicken coop, pigsty, stable, and hayloft was transformed into four motel-like bedrooms, each with a mezzanine and a bed above a sitting room furnished with French doors opening onto the garden.

From such a setting in the forest, one would expect a country décor. However, the color scheme and the Scandinavian-style furniture exude a refinement that stands out in this feral setting. White is the dominant color, with faded and flaking sky-blue accenting the door and the window frames and which is seen again, in varying shades, on the antique furniture. The great charm of this unusual refuge is, without a doubt, the view from the large bay windows in each room—woods in every direction. Dawn brings the company of deer and rabbits to those most discreet spaces. ❧

Left: Found through-out—whether as small dabs of color on most of the doors and window frames, or on the contemporary furniture and some of the old pieces—an icy blue tone is part of the charm of this house. It bestows a subtle freshness somewhat in contrast to the country atmosphere and creates an ambience of well-being and a gentle way of life.

Right: Mushrooms and pinecones, zinc and terra-cotta objects speak of nature.

Above left: In the attic bedroom, the country style comes out in the solid oak floor, with its boards of variable widths, the Swedish wood-burning stove, and the portrait of a hunter, a work by the master of the house.

Above right: The same monochrome gray-blue is seen on the Louis XVI chair, the quilt, and the watercolors.

A small mid-twentieth-century Russian painting, *Lunch Under the Pergola*, echoes the garden life and the ambience of summer under the oak trees and near the arbor. The furniture in the sitting room, all white and intentionally discreet, leaves the limelight to a pair of eighteenth-century cabinets.

Variations on the Past

Left: Atop the blood-red Louis XV chest of drawers, sits a pair of eighteenth-century flame vases and a watch holder. The painting, *La jeune femme au jardin* (*The Young Woman in the Garden*), is a self-portrait by the painter Corrine Forgot.

Top right: In the bedroom, the mistress of the house has used Jouy fabrics along with cloth from Nantes of the same color for the bed skirts and bed-tester.

Top left: For the guest bedroom, she chose the blond woods of this English furniture. The openwork cane chair dates from the eighteenth century.

ifteen years ago, a young Parisian antiques dealer fell madly in love with a pretty manor house that was built in 1735 by an Anjou country squire. The house bore an unusual history: At the beginning of the nineteenth century, a viticulturist set up business there and it flourished to such an extent that he made his enterprise into a "model farm." Even today, some of his avant-garde farming machines are on exhibit at a regional museum.

Almost a century later, a new owner moved in with his wife and four daughters. A company director on the cutting edge for his time and a great hydraulics enthusiast, he installed cistern towers to collect the rainwater, which he then used for central heating and hot water in the bathrooms. According to his plans, his four daughters would give him eight grandchildren, so he divided all the rooms in the house in preparation for the future little ones. Two of the four daughters took to the veil, a third remained single, but the fourth saved the day and astonishingly gave him twelve grandchildren. His already optimistic projections so grandly surpassed, in 1927 he added another floor to the building, but by then he had also gotten it into his head to house his vineyard workers.

And so it is to this special setting in the heart of the Anjou countryside that this young Parisian antiques dealer returns every week, as she spends weekends at her antiques stall in the Paul-Bert de Saint-Ouen market.

In addition to her passion for antiques, she also loves decorating, and Laurence took charge of the restoration of this mansion, subdivided by her predecessor. The entire interior had to be reconceived, breaking down all the partitions and returning the space to its previous elegant dimensions.

The mistress of this estate works from the heart, by feel, and without preconceived notions. The eighteenth and nineteenth centuries coexist with the charm and rhythm of her discoveries. This mélange of beloved objects that she has assembled over the years seems as if it has always been there. Just as in old family houses, they have become the memory of the place where an atmosphere of perpetual vacation and gaiety reigns as befits the landlady. ✃

Far left: In the kitchen, the dinnerware is stored on wood and blackened metal industrial shelving.

Left: The metal clothing frame and chair in the child's bedroom were found while hunting for antiques.

Right: Placed beneath the window, this meridienne sofa, covered in a reproduction of a Jouy fabric, is ideal for dreaming or reading.

Beneath a crystal
pendant chandelier,
the garden pedestal
table stands next to
an Empire table and
chairs and in front of
a nineteenth-century
decorative screen.

A Napoléon III
stand and its elegant
Empire vase of
painted metal appear
silhouetted before
the background of
English-green wood
paneling.

The Attics of Stockholm

In the garrets of an old building in Stockholm, the designer Martine Colliander has renovated a stunning space devoted to the color white, ad infinitum. Any question of color yields but one response: white. But white, too, has it nuances.

The walls are white, the floors and rugs are white, the Gustavian furniture is white, as are most of the objects, the bed linens, and the dishes. Only a few traces of aquamarine remind the inhabitants that the sea is just steps away.

The capital of Sweden is, in fact, built on fourteen islands of an archipelago that comprises more than twenty thousand islands. In the soul of every Swede resides a sailor. As soon as spring arrives, the residents of Stockholm have only one thought in mind—a weekend getaway on an island.

After completing her studies in psychology and sociology, disciplines she continues to pursue, Martine created a collection of Gustavian-style furniture—chairs, dressers, buffets, and chests of drawers—perfect replicas of the eighteenth-century Swedish style. Sold at White on White, the Lexington Avenue shop in New York, the line has been a great success.

A loyal devotee of old linens, Martine launched White Sense—a collection of household linens and clothes hand-embroidered in India—five years ago. Continuing to work as a decorator, she and two friends recently opened Oscar and Clothilde in Stockholm. Along with Martine's own collections, including countless objects she has brought back from her travels to all corners of the world, the friends sell French and Swedish antiques.

Between shuttling back and forth, Martine has moved into an apartment situated in the attic of an early nineteenth-century Stockholm building. Although not well decorated, it holds great potential. In order to create an "open space," she took down all the non-supporting walls, as well as the false ceiling, and exposed the structure of this *torkvin*. In olden days, here amid the convergence of the chimneys, the residents from the floors below would dry their laundry. The dominant factor throughout the apartment remains white, even if there is some variation between the patinas of the furniture, the tone of the linens, the cotton of the curtains, the fabric of the sofas, and the hue of the faience dishware. ❧

Left: All the chimneys in this Swedish building converge in the attic, making it possible to open up the space. Beauty, simplicity, and functionality are the three ruling principles. The kitchen island was made from small stones and the work surface from sand tiles.

Right: Next to the chimney is a reproduction of a Pompeii fresco done by Jonas Wikman, titled *Odile la servante* (*Odile the Servant*).

Left: The view of the gardens and the black roofs of the Swedish capital are striking. The duckboard terrace is made from odd pieces of wood and the salvaged furniture has been whitewashed.

Right: A majestic pair of eighteenth-century doors, found at an antiques shop, open onto an attic bedroom. Books are stacked on a simple white folding table; on the bed are pieces from the owner's collection of house linens. On the windowsill sits a pot of *marbächas*, Swedish geraniums renowned for their incomparable pale-pink hue.

Preceding pages: In front of the second terrace, the dining room is furnished with a garden table bought in Paris and chairs from Martine's collection. Beside the fireplace, aligned with the edge of the enormous chimney, hangs a pair Edvard Munch self-portraits. The various plaster casts were found at secondhand shops.

Far left: Sometimes the simplest of ideas makes for a pretty decoration, like this postcard of Vermeer's *Girl with a Pearl Earring* glued onto a tile.

Above left: Above the austere console composed of blocks of cement supported on a metal structure, hangs Petter Claeson's painting, a nod to the contemporary. The plaster cast was found at a Brussels flea market.

Life as an Antiques Hunter

From mother to daughter, and from daughter to granddaughter: The antiquing gene is not recessive in this family. Quite early on, this daughter of an antiques dealer followed her mother along the secondhand road. Nathalie Besnard's dream was to open a shop right near her home, as her mother had done.

And so, in the old village of Soisy-sur-Seine south of Paris, along a wide avenue bordered by acacias, she discovered this 1900 buhrstone villa situated in the middle of a 21,500-square-foot (2,000-square-meter) garden that even had a pretty little orangery.

The renovation turned out to be easy. The oak parquet floors were kept in all the rooms and

only the 1950s tile floor in the entryway was replaced with stone from Burgundy and black cabochons, which was more in keeping with the style of decoration.

The attic had never been finished and was completely insulated and floored with planks of raw pine that were painted a pearly gray, as were the

Left: Next to an Alsatian clock, its yellow patina carefully restored, an eighteenth-century mirror with a gilded wooden frame hangs above a small table covered with objects, including a miniature sedan-chair.

Right: In the foyer of the house, a ceramic wood-burning stove hailing from eastern France serves as a pretty stand for a stuffed duck. On the wall, next to an eighteenth-century portrait of a woman and above a cane chair, hangs a rain-worn decorative plaster garden piece.

Left: The girl's bedroom is decorated in a harmonious composition of painted furniture and antique toys with a pair of wooden shutters in the corner.

Right: A soft gray dominates the bedroom. A baldachin made from an eighteenth-century printed calico crowns a simple pair of Louis XVI wooden headboards. The bed is covered in white lace bedding.

Far right: The two basins, found in some old water closets, were reunited in this bathroom. The legs have been hidden behind cotton drapes purchased in Sweden.

beams. A bedroom was set up and, using the beams as a natural partition, a quasi-separate sitting area was created there beneath the rafters.

As the little orangery at the back of the garden was too dilapidated to be restored, it is now being used as a charming toolshed and a perfectly ventilated storeroom for the apples and pears from the orchard.

This antiques hunter does not let a good deal go by. One morning, she picked up a set of old shutters that had been left on the sidewalk by a demolition crew.

The shop was opened in an outbuilding where she regularly displays arrangements of eighteenth- and nineteenth-century furniture and objects.

Perhaps one day the torch will be once again passed from mother to daughter. Laurie, who often joins the antiques hunt, is particularly fond of old fabrics, which now fill the dresser drawers in her bedroom.

Preceding pages: In the dining room, a rare Directoire metal soup tureen sits atop a table covered with a quilt. A shop cabinet serves as a breakfront. On the Louis XV buffet, a showcase is filled with gilded wooden and zinc objects.

Left: In the sitting room, atop a Louis XVI stone mantelpiece, a pair of Italian candlesticks saved from the owners' previous home bookends a Directoire soup tureen. The fireplace is framed by two wooden shutters found on the street.

Right: A pretty arrangement of nineteenth-century masters in a harmonious natural palette hangs above the sofa. In the foreground is a gilded wood plinth from a church statue.

The Second Life of a Family Home

Left and bottom right:
In the kitchen, three
large beams support
whitewashed joists.
The glass showcase
from a seed
merchant's shop,
used to store dishes,
stands on a floor
made of cement tiles.
Both the lattice doors
and the shelves are
natural wood; only
the wood frame of the
back service entrance
has been painted
gray. A zinc horse's
head, a sign from a
butcher shop, hangs
on the wall. Next to
the étagère filled with
both functional and
decorative glass jars,
above the built-in
stove, some finials are
displayed.

Following pages:
In the bathroom, an
old shop counter has
been used as a base
for the white marble
surface. Surrounded
by two zinc mirrors,
the oeil-de-boeuf lets
light into the facing
landing.

$\mathcal{D}$uring a walk through the Savoy countryside, Patrick and Véronique Bellemin were drawn to a solid eighteenth-century building that, with its façade of white and ocher stripes, was typical of the regional architecture. Some time after their first visit, they found themselves seduced by the thousands of details. Along with its original façade, the lapping water in the stone pool, the scallop-tiled roof, and the old lacy wooden balcony soon won them over. Real estate agents in Chambéry, the Bellemins found the location of this house to be ideal: near the city, but in the middle of the hills, the mountains on the horizon.

Originally, the main house was independent from the outbuilding; however, finding the former too small for their family, they decided to build an annex between the two existing parts. In order to integrate the new structure, they used the same materials as in the older parts and built the same quadri-sloped scallop-tiled roof. The impression is that the extension, which gives the property a certain majestic air, has always been there.

Major renovations were required. Only the small sitting room remains as it was, while a better oriented, contemporary-style sitting room was created in the new part. The kitchen is reached by climbing a few steps and passing through old greenhouse doors, which were salvaged from a scrap dealer specializing in antique materials. The second floor was completely redone with the installation of two bathrooms, a laundry room, and five spacious bedrooms, each with views of the countryside. Without altering the soul of the house, another generation has breathed new life into it. ❧

Above left: The bed, set on a floor of old *tomettes,* has a Louis XVI–style doored night table on either side that has been stripped to its original patina.

Above right: A baroque double bed with sculpted angels has just had a wash of color.

Above right:
The walls of the sitting room have been whitewashed. The Louis XV–style console set in front of pine paneling is framed by a pair of sculpted wooden candelabras. On the marble tabletop stand a shrine and a seventeenth-century candlestick that has been made into a lamp.

The Past as a Point of Reference

Immediately upon leaving the city, one is in the heart of the country. Philippe and Isabelle Guémard, both natives of Angers, chose to make their home a few minutes from the town center so they could live and work in the open countryside.

La Tour ("The Tower"), dating from the mid-eighteenth century, was the deciding factor. Passed from hand to hand since the end of the nineteenth century, La Tour was home to a ship's captain, then a local writer, then a soap factory before finding itself in the expert hands of these antiques decorators.

As it was in very poor condition, the house required major restoration. Only one concession to modernity was made—a metal staircase (salvaged from an old factory) was installed to replace a dilapidated wooden staircase that led to the next floor. The rest of the house is entirely devoted to eighteenth-century style, of which both Guémards are fervent proponents. They have also opened a shop in an outbuilding, and they often move furniture back and forth between to see how it looks until they place it permanently.

On the second floor, the large rooms have the luxury of double exposure. The coffered ceiling and parquet floors are original. The heavily draped windows are furnished with interior shutters. The sun continually streams through the slightly irregular old glass panes of the wide facing windows. The subtle affinity of the objects, the simplicity and artistry of the inspired composition present a blend of formality and abundance, richness and sobriety, great charm and elegance. ❧

Left and right:
An astronomical telescope, candlesticks and candelabra, framed plant illustrations, an antique cage, a bell lantern, and a crystal pendant chandelier — all found in second-hand shops—bring the past back to life.

Following pages:
This sitting room brings a return to the eighteenth century with its period fireplace, a Louis XV "confidant" sofa (so named for its angled seats), and a duchesse chair divided into three parts, which form a meridienne sofa when set together.

Left: To join kitchen onto the entryway, the doors and separating walls have been replaced by a shop counter. The old tiles were found at a salvager's shop, and the sink, made of slate from the region, came from a house under demolition.

Right: A series of lovely reception rooms leads to the dining room. Its unusual white-painted staircase blends in with the rest of the furnishings. Around the refectory table are reproductions of Louis XV chairs.

A Small Space and Grand Ideas

Left: The bookcases
were built around
the 1900 fireplace
in order to house
a veritable curio
collection of
thoroughly charming
objects: a twelfth-
century wooden
processional Virgin,
rebound antiquarian
books, a cast-iron
lion's head, artists'
models, quills,
glass globes,
boxwood flasks for
traveling, Medici
vases, an ostrich
egg, lead soldiers,
a collection of boxes
of theater sequins,
and antique toys.

In the back of a small Parisian courtyard, there was an ordinary nineteenth-century house with an unused attic. One day, the landlord of the top floor got an idea to enlarge her 325-square-foot (30-square-meter) apartment. The attic, situated directly above, could be opened up, and her apartment, overnight, would be transformed into a château with thirteen-foot (four-meter) ceilings! This is precisely what Corrine Porte, an antiques dealer by trade and used to the large interiors of her beautiful old family house, decided to do. After a minimum amount of renovation—the cement floor was simply covered over with a birch veneer—she set about lending the apartment the feel of a family house, no mean feat. To create the ambiance she so loved, she designed a huge bookcase to frame the classic early twentieth-century black marble fireplace, and then filled it with old rebound books and all sorts of objects—statues, candlesticks, lamps—that she had found here and there. She decided to place her bedroom on a mezzanine in the more intimate space of the attic which, just as in the old days, is accessed by a wooden ladder. ❧

Left: A section of the attic was retained and transformed into a loft bedroom that is accessed by a carpenter's ladder.

Above: This eighteenth-century screen reveals, panel by panel, the lively scene of a fishing port in full swing.

Left: This chandelier with glass votives is a replica of one found in the Saint Sophia Basilica in Istanbul. Near the window is a trompe-l'oeil of Delft dishes, which is surrounded by the real thing.

A Decorator in a Haussmann Apartment

These bookcases have been objects of particular attention from the mistress of the home. Set in a row above the upper wainscoting and the height of a small book, the elements flow in cadence with the moldings. The design of the lower part was inspired by the gently curved ceiling cornice. The placement of the chairs was determined by the moldings.

A little less than a hundred years ago, a well-advised landlord could buy an apartment of good standing in Paris by selling off a few dozen cows from his herd (in this case, fifty fine Limousin cows). Not everyone was taken by this bright idea, but that was what a certain Arsène did, the grandfather of the current landlords. And good that he did.

Since then, several generations of Parisians have been born here, just a stone's throw from the Arc de Triomphe, in what is called a "family apartment," as though there were many others throughout the capital. Descendants of pirates from the region of Saint-Malo, they remain quite attached to those parts. Family members have been born in these bedrooms, and often they have died in the same ones.

Furnished with pieces passed down from generation to generation, the atmosphere has evolved

thanks to the current mistress of the house, a designer by profession. Trained in the school of one of the most famous designers, Primrose Bordier, she is versed in all subtle harmonies and knows perfectly how to assemble objects by their affinities, colors, materials, and relationships. Working in the studios of Parisian magazines, she has been applying this acumen for years with an innate feel for composition and a passion that has yet to ebb.

Not too long ago, in the foyer, which looks onto an inner courtyard, there had been a beautiful stained-glass window that still had its original panes of pink and green foliage. Accidentally broken, it was replaced by tall, small-paned windows in the same Haussmann style that allow a pretty light to fill the foyer. Thanks to an ingenious plant stand construction kit, a kind of interior garden was created in which morning glories can climb and geraniums can blossom protected from the cold. It took true talent to give an original tone to this very classic interior, so close to one of the world's most beautiful boulevards—the Champs-Élysées. ❧

Left: A typical Haussmann-style fireplace. This family counts some pirates among its ancestors, and a portrait of one of them is simply set upon the octagonal Louis XIII table. Between the sofa and the Loom chairs is a low table covered with art books and a bowl filled with antique decorated balls, collected by the mistress of the home.

Right: This eighteenth-century black crossbow chest of drawers is placed in the hallway that opens onto the dining room.

Left: More than any other room in the house, this bedroom is a reliquary of memories. Childhood photographs, a fob watch, ivory bracelets, pill boxes, snuffboxes, and dance cards have been arranged with great care on a platter and in baskets.

Right: One of the assets of this apartment is undoubtedly its magnificent hardwood oak floors laid in a chevron pattern. The aroma of fine wax and the reflected sunlight streaming through the tall windows of each room add to the atmosphere.

A House with a Vagabond Feel

wo houses side by side, almost twins, separated by a garden. We are a half-hour from Paris, near Étampes. In this hilly countryside within the Beauce region, the village of Mesnil-Girault, not more than a hamlet, sits lost in the wheat fields. While their numbers are continually diminishing, a few farms do remain, and it is on one of these that Martine has made her home and opened an antiques shop called the Marquis de Carabas.

It is difficult to differentiate between the shop and the home, not only because the two are so sim-ilar in construction, but also because they are both filled with eighteenth-century furniture and objects. It is not uncommon for some couch or table to make the trip back and forth between the two buildings until finding its proper place.

Over the years, the two stories of the principal residence had required serious renovations, including painting, plumbing, and electricity, and the owners decided to do all the work themselves. Some of the narrow windows were replaced with bay windows to bring more light into this house, which had been somewhat dark due to the construction typi-

cal of a period when walls were thick and openings small to protect from the heat, as well as from the cold. On the ground floor, the old floor tiles (*tomettes*) and the exposed beams were preserved. On one side of the garden, a whitewashed barn served as the summer reception room. This has become a shop, as has a second house, between the seesaw and the goldfish pond, in the shade of the weeping willows.

The garden, per se, did not exist. It had been a true virgin forest left to the whims of the invading nature. After a major clearing, trees and bushes were harmoniously distributed around the two houses, immersing them in greenery. Twenty-five years later, the fine earth of Beauce has given the trees the appearance of being hundreds of years old, which in turn, accord summertime lunches an opportune shade. ❧

Left: The panes of this cupboard have been replaced by fine, wire-reinforced glass. One of the masterfully handmade bookcases is topped with an adapted pediment from a mirror. Another holds Creil, Pontaux-Choux, and Sarreguemines faience, and a third is replete with objects and books, creating a warm ambiance.

Right: A gentle
harmony of antique
tones reigns over
this dinnerware
with octagonal
Creil faience plates
complemented
by fringed
monogrammed
napkins.

Right: The walls of this house have exposed stones. Two nineteenth-century candelabras are set atop a pretty antique piece of embroidery used as a tablecloth. The wall is decorated with a contemporary painting with a classical spirit and several old watercolors and drawings.

Above: Beneath the canopy of the house, guests are welcomed into a country ambiance with the collection of antique birdcages that hang here and there. A nursing chair is next to a rustic buffet, and an old Brazilian bench brims with cans and milk pots filled with wild flowers.

Above: This Louis XV sofa is covered with a Jouy fabric. The bay window is adorned with the pediment from a patinated armoire, as is the bookshelf.

The Fancies of a Learned Woman

When one is so thoroughly possessed by the antiques demon, two houses are a necessity, not a luxury. One for living, the other for working, and both to assuage a passion—an unbridled love and fascination for eighteenth-century style. Accustomed to living in a refined environment ever since childhood, Sophie Prételat acquired a taste for antique furniture and beautiful objects.

Located in Anjou in the heart of France, the two houses are only a few miles apart along a small winding street through the countryside. This antiques dealer lives in the first house and applies her decorating talents by laying out arrangements of unusual eighteenth- and nineteenth-century objects in the second. She does, however, also spend the year crisscrossing the French provinces in search of the rare gems that she chooses not for their commercial value, nor even their aesthetic appeal. "All that matters is that the object has an *esprit.*"

In the estate she shares with members of her family, she has decorated her living quarters with some of her unseen finds, recreating an atmosphere typical of the eighteenth century, yet peppered with her talent, humor, and whimsy. In the residence, which is more than three centuries old, as in her house boutique Anges et Démons and in the homes she decorates, she enjoys relentlessly composing still lifes inspired by "curio cabinets" which are highly evocative of the Age of Enlightenment—so many scenes, free-form in nature—with enchanting results.

She is wonderfully adept at sustaining this unique, inspired, and seductive ambiance, arranging hunting trophies with balusters, plaster, and zinc objects, garden bells, herbaria, fossils, masterworks, herbalists' bottles, mercury lamps, millefiori glass paperweights, soft furnishings, and charming lace work. Each piece finds new life in these décors, which at times can be bold, but always successful. Both in her home and the boutique, she offers an ongoing lesson in style. ❧

Left: This cherrywood two-part breakfront is a veritable curio cabinet. The antiquarian botanical books share space with seashells, two *paludiers* (winter seasonal workers in salt marshes), a shark's jaw, an artist's model, bottles of leeches, eighteenth-century Provençal *santons,* and an enamel pinecone from an Italian garden. The top is crowned with a seagull, two papier-mâché theatrical helmets, a globe of the earth, and a leather-covered wooden horse.

Right: The bookcase was made from sections of eighteenth-century paneling stripped and left raw. Set among the books is a Sicilian marionette and glass paperweights. An eighteenth-century architect's table displays a lamp with a sculpted wood stem, a statue's missing hand, a Nuremberg articulated doll, and painted metal cages.

Above: The Italian wooden bedsteads, on which once perched sculpted eagles, have been repatinated. The baldachin was fashioned from a roof frieze that came from a family house; on the wall is a collection of framed eighteenth- and nineteenth-century embroideries. The mirror, with its gilded wooden sculpted angels, dates from the seventeenth century. The bedding is made of Jouy fabric.

Above left:
The bathroom is covered in red-and-white striped wallpaper. In front of the window are a barber's table and a swing mirror made of turned wood.

Above right:
A seventeenth-century processional statue in her silk brocade finery is illuminated by the sunlight. An eighteenth-century multicolored wooden statuette of a saint sits atop a capital.

Above left:
A collection of
Directoire apothecary
jars, herbalist's jars,
and a set of Creil
faience dishes are

displayed on the
narrow shelves of
this black bookcase.

Above right: Amid the
woodwork and the
columns painted in
trompe-l'oeil, a bust
of the twentieth-
century figure Charles

Vedry is framed by a
pair of Medici vases
with odd bouquets.

Above left and right:
Near the window, a copy
of a nineteenth-century
bust of Emperor Caracalla
keeps company with a
processional Virgin Mary
and Child.

Following pages:
The artist's spirit
wafts through this
room. On the walls
are maps, drawings,
right angles, and
masterworks, while
on the low table are
silvered glass balls.

Top left: On the mantelpiece are a stone lion and a lamp fashioned from a baluster. The bookcase also brims with decoration: heads from milliners' dummies, toys, and other historical objects.

Bottom left: The blood-red walls of the sitting room set off the black armoire from Uzès on which are displayed a pair of glass bell jars and an unusual collection of seashells. To the left is a seventeenth-century breakfront made of larch wood, decorated in trompe-l'oeil. The nineteenth-century fruitwood marriage table with twisted legs comes from eastern France.

Right: Beneath a portrait depicting one of the children Marie Leszczynska and Louis XV is a bride in her glass house and an eighteenth-century satin brocade garter belt displayed atop an eighteenth-century chest of drawers done in marquetry.

Left: Displayed with a collection of seaweed and shell creations is an exceptional work on butterflies.

Right: An eighteenth-century chest of drawers and mirror are placed next to a Directoire Lorraine chair decorated with a landscape painted on metal and *arte povera* boxes.

Far right: Originally a decorative garden piece, this zinc agave is displayed with a sculpted wooden head on the slate surface of a chest of drawers.

The Eighteenth Century, Free-Form

Given carte blanche to redecorate entirely a large apartment in one of Paris's finest districts, the interior architect Jean-François Millevoye immediately set off on a total transformation of this space, emblematic of early twentieth-century French architecture. As he explained, "I thought, in complete agreement with my clients, that the majestic and unusual proportions were poorly served by the razzamatazz of moldings, rosettes, festoons, and other flowery ornamentations that were everywhere along the perimeters and in the center of the ceilings. I know that these are normally considered the end-all, but we wanted a greater degree of sobriety. On the other hand, the great height of the ceilings, the spectacular foyer, and the large reception rooms were irresistible."

A recognized specialist of the Age of Enlightenment, this decorator had been drawn to the decorative arts from a very early age. The son of a developer, he was in the habit of copying his father's blueprints (after having first finished his homework) and loved visiting museums, where he was particularly attracted to sculptures.

Millevoye conceived a rather revolutionary project for this apartment, replacing the classic double doors with simple floor-to-ceiling openings, skillfully working the perspectives and increasing the number of hallways. From each point of entry, as well as from the sitting room and from the dining room, the eye takes off in several directions, coming to rest on several planes. "The true luxury remains. It is the volumes, the height, the setting, which all push the limits of these huge spaces to the maximum."

By painting a tall and narrow corridor apple green, he managed to create a strong decorative element bravely married to the eggplant-colored walls of the library. He also took excruciating care in the choice of each accessory, such as the doorknobs and the radiator covers made from security gates set in old, stripped floorboards that had first been stained cherry red and then waxed, as had been done with all the floors throughout the apartment. He also designed a stunning bookcase made out of Portuguese slate, not to mention the extraordinary finishing work of the walls, which he did according to very old techniques perfected by repetition. In some areas, parts of the building structure were exposed to enhance the contemporary feel of the place, taking it down to the bare essentials, with neither fanfare nor pretense. By bringing the space up-to-date, the solemn atmosphere of a Florentine palace was achieved. ✃

Left and right: Three sculptures by Roland Damien are seen in the foreground. The dining table has been fashioned out of elements from a late-nineteenth-century factory. The chairs are reproductions of the Gustavian period. The pair of buffets is made from a set of eighteenth-century Provençal wood paneling.

Following pages:
In order to install
the bookcase, the wall
had to be cut and then
buttressed by four
layers of lumber. The
shelves have been
framed in Spanish
slate and set in
mitered angles. The
painting is by Pierre
Gaste.

Above left: A very solid slab of Spanish slatework surface has been posed on the white-leaded oak elements.

Above right: In the bathroom, the walls are *tadelak* (a Moroccan form of whitewash plaster) and smooth clay mounted in alternation. The floor is stained and polished cement. Atop the garden table is an eighteenth-century frame used for a mirror.

Right: In the hallway, some exposed bricks have been framed in steel and set behind frosted glass.

Northern Lights in the Île-de-France

One day, with no regrets, they turned the page and left behind their comfortable home for three semi-abandoned little houses near the church in a traditional old village. "Village life held great appeal to us. Our last house was far from everything and was surrounded by large estates. Here, you live like in the old days, walking to all the shops. We know everyone and everyone knows us. It's such a pleasure to live our days in the rhythm of the chiming church bells, where there are so many hardworking students, and on Sundays to hear the singing of the Mass from the house. It's another life."

In the foothills that once flaunted grapevines, the Saint-Vincent abode that dates to the mid-seventeenth century had initially been a presbytery before becoming a barn for storing tithes, which it remained until the Revolution.

Three centuries later, on the same foothills now planted with apple trees, three rather dilapidated houses were dying of boredom. With the help of an architect, the new landlords renovated them from top to bottom. To provide as much leeway as possible for a complete restructuring of the interior spaces, only the supporting walls and structure were retained. The result is a custom-built new house that is both comfortable and functional. Using only old materials that had been salvaged, the new owners were able to recapture the soul of the old buildings, which was of utmost importance to them. The garden, which had been on an extreme slope, was terraced, creating several more easily accessible levels and also making it possible to install a swimming pool that would not be seen from the sitting room.

The construction completed, all that remained was the decoration—a passion of the mistress of the house. With the help of a friend who is both a specialist in eighteenth-century style and an avid shopper, she found tables, couches, desks, candelabras, pastels, and other accessories that bestow upon the space both an elegance of yesteryear and the comforts of today. ✂

Page 253: A Louis XVI–period day bed, with a garden pedestal table on either side, welcomes guests into the home. The floor is made of stones from Burgundy and laid with pink cabochons.

Right: The grand double staircase, designed by an architect, separates the dining room to the north and the sitting room to the south. A set of painted wooden baluster lamps of various sizes is beneath the oeil-de-boeuf. The pendant chandelier hangs above a table around which a set of Louis XIII–style chairs are covered in linen.

Left: There are many
French doors, which
open on one side onto
the village square and
onto the garden on
the other side.

Right: Throughout
the house, the
parquet floor is
made of wide blond
oak slats that create
a sense of unity. The
kitchen is illuminated
by two crystal
chandeliers; the
dining area is
furnished with a
nineteenth-century
reproduction of a
rustic Louis XV table
and Louis XVI chairs.
A rare artesian piece
with a two-level
surface stands
against the wall.

Far right: In the
sitting room, situated
in front of a Louis
XVI–period stone
fireplace adorned
by a pediment, a
small area has been
designed around a
garden pedestal table
and two chairs of the
same period.

The low table in
the sitting room
was made from
eighteenth-century
oak flooring and
mounted on a wooden
base. The breakfront,
which still bears its
original paint, is
from the Bordeaux
region. This rather
rare piece, with its
two pairs of doors, is
ideal for displaying
both dinnerware and
antiquarian books.
Next to the Louis
XVI–style sofa stands
a floor lamp that is a
composite of several
antique parts.

The monochrome
green shelves, the
bindings of the books,
and the "Trianon"
Badonviller faience
dining service make
a pretty tableau.

Far right: The bathroom is constructed in whitened planks of raw wood. This style of bathtub, with its lion's-claw feet, has become ever more popular. Sunlight streams through the two eaved windows.

Right: In the bedroom, four partially stripped wooden shutters serve as the headboard for the bed, over which a blood-red wooden frame and a pair of eighteenth-century engravings have been hung as decoration.

Exercises in Style

Preceding page:
A 1940s metal chest from a dentist's office is accompanied by an eighteenth-century oak bed-tester with sculpted cherubs and a magnificent piece of coral. The mélange of such disparate objects creates a bold arrangement.

Left: Through the half-opened door of the painted wooden Provençal bookcase, a collection of corals, some of which have been mounted, are displayed beneath a set of plated glasses.

Far right: In the bedroom, a late-seventeenth-century *mazot* door from a Swiss mountain storehouse is used as a headboard.

It is through his passion for nature—which was awakened during the long days of his childhood spent in his grandmother's garden—that Stéphane Olivier, an antiques dealer by trade, explains his professional odyssey. "It was the birth of all my senses, the point of departure for all my emotions. I was born with a garden at the bottom of my heart."

Thus, it is not surprising to find him in the middle of the Saint-Ouen flea market, in "the little house," an extremely rare, albeit modest 1900 buhrstone villa surrounded by a grandmother's garden. Along the gravel paths protected by a bamboo hedge, stone geese sit among the watering cans, birdcages, and cast-metal pedestal tables overflowing with objects. It is certainly the garden that sets the tone for the whole spread.

Entering the house—that is, the shop on the ground floor—the same spirit prevails. Every room is inundated with statues, sculptures, trophies, monumental terra-cotta pieces, and furniture. While the patinas of some have been worn away by the weather, their organized presentation radiates an extraordinary power of seduction. A rare and romantic atmosphere pervades. The visitor, with the look of a flabbergasted child, discovers a strange and unreal world—the world of Alice in Wonderland. The private apartments on the second floor exhibit the same inspiration. The master of the house replaced the wallpaper with nine coats of paint made from natural pigments. Entering his bedroom is like walking into a curio cabinet, and the bathroom bursts with the same charm. Not a single room escapes the magic of his talent.

Stéphane Olivier recently opened a second shop in the heart of Saint-Germain-des-Prés. ✢

Left: A marine atmosphere pervades the bathroom, with its display of corals and seaweed.

Right: In a zinc pail, daffodils and buttercups glisten in the sunlight in front of a collection of corals set on a garden table. An army of plated candlesticks stands at attention on the shelves of the buffet. The chandelier is an original montage of antique wooden elements with decorative pendants. A halo for the cast angel was once part of a fountain.

Above left: This credenza from the Haute-Savoie region, with its pretty mix of solid and paned doors, displays a faience dining service from the Belgian royal family.

Above right: A 1920s work of marquetry in chestnut wood and a sliver-plated screen with a bamboo motif are examples of extraordinarily fine craftsmanship.

Above left: Sitting on a staircase landing, this bull's head, once a sign for a butcher shop, seems decidedly huge. Its horns brush up against an Austrian cast-iron coatrack from the early nineteenth century. The painting, *Le joueur de flûte* (*The Flute Player*), is from the same period.

Above right: This mottled-paint surface was attained by a thermal stripping process.

Address Book

Emmanuel San Martino and
Christophe Hervé
Odorantes
9 Rue Madame
75006 Paris, France
Tel. + 33 (0) 1 42 84 03 00

Peter Gabriëlse (France)
Tel./Fax + 33 (0) 2 33 64 27 12

Stephan and Paola Söder (Sweden)
Tel. + 46 (0) 8 54 35 43 41

Françoise Manceau is
opening a store in Paris.
Mobile + 33 (0) 6 12 08 58 01

Fabrice Diomard
L'autre Maison
54 Avenue de La Motte-Picquet
75015 Paris, France
Tel. + 33 (0) 1 45 67 68 07
Mobile + 33 (0) 6 14 17 11 35
fabrice.diomard@laposte.net

Chantal Vautrelle
Vautrelle Gervaise
La Verglasserie le Pin
73240 Gresin, France
Tel. + 33 (0) 4 76 32 50 49 or 31 72 06
Mobile + 33 (0) 6 84 50 61 80

Elisabeth Brac de La Perrière
Vert de Gris
6 Rue Ernest Deloison
92200 Neuilly sur Seine, France
Tel. + 33 (0) 1 47 38 64 89
Mobile + 33 (0) 6 22 86 40 43

Marcel Marongiu
www.marcelmarongiu.com

Laure du Chatenet
Maison Caumont
35 Avenue Victor Hugo
75116 Paris, France
Tel. + 33 (0) 1 44 17 94 04
www.caumont-antiques.com
contact@caumont-antiques.com

Château d'Outrelaise
14680 Gouvix, France
Tel. + 33 (0) 2 31 23 86 81 or 79 03 64
www.outrelaise.com

Woody Biggs and Stephen Shubel
(France and USA)
Tel. France + 33 (0) 2 41 57 15 08
Tel. California + 1 415 332 8008

Cléo Burtin
Boutique Antiquités
26 Rue Paul Séramy
77300 Fontainebleau, France
Mobile + 33 (0) 6 71 20 15 02
or + 33 (0) 6 07 24 78 65

Laurence Lenglare
110 Rue des Rosiers
93400 Puces de Saint Ouen, France
Tel. + 33 (0) 1 40 11 91 47
Mobile + 33 (0) 6 80 71 91 89

Martine Colliander
Oscar and Clothilde
Nybrogätan 7
114 34 Stockholm, Sweden
Tel. + 46 (0) 8611 53 00
www.oscarclothilde.com
oscar@oscarclothilde.com

Nathalie Besnard
La Petite Fadette
32 Blvd. de la République
91450 Soisy-sur-Seine, France
Tel. + 33 (0) 1 60 75 76 77
Mobile + 33 (0) 6 68 29 05 69

Phillippe and Isabelle Guémard
Rendez-vous
5 Promenade de la Baumette
49000 Angers, France
Tel. + 33 (0) 2 41 86 85 88
rendez-vous@cegetel.net

Corinne Porte
Porte de Vanves
75014 Paris, France
Mobile + 33 (0) 6 16 70 59 37

Martine Ouvrard and Olivier Peffau
Le Marquis de Carabas
Le Mesnil-Girault,
91690 Boissy la Rivière, France
Tel. + 33 (0) 1 64 94 88 57
Mobile + 33 (0) 6 84 21 61 39

Sophie Prételat
Anges et Démons
4 Rue de l'Eglise
49150 Baugé, France
Mobile + 33 (0) 6 03 56 09 26

J.F. Millevoye, Antique-Interior
Architecture (France)
Tel + 33 (0) 6 89 25 76 76
jfcmillevoye@noos.fr

Stéphane Olivier
3 Rue de l'Université
75007 Paris, France
Tel. + 33 (0) 1 42 96 10 00
rivegauche@stephaneolivier.fr
La Petite Maison
10 Rue Paul Bert
93400 Saint Ouen, France
Tel. + 33 (0) 1 40 10 56 69

To Amable, Frédéric and Françoise, Aurélie and Olivier.

To Corine, Louise, and Manon.

The authors deeply thank everyone who has helped in the achievement of this book by opening their doors to their homes, and especially Annie-Camille Kuentzmann and Sophie Prételat for their precious help.

They also would like to express their gratitude to Henri Bovet for his knowledgeable advice and to the team at La Martinière, Brigitte Govignon and Audrey Demarre, who were in charged of the production of this work.

Project Manager, English-language edition: Magali Veillon
Copy-editor, English-language edition: Aiah Wieder, with Eti Bonn-Muller
Designer, English-language edition: Shawn Dahl, with Neil Egan
Jacket design, English-language edition: E.Y. Lee
Production Manager, English-language edition: Colin Hough Trapp

Library of Congress Cataloging-in-Publication Data
Lalande, Michèle.
The new eighteenth-century style : rediscovering a French décor /
text by Michèle Lalande ; photographs by Gilles Trillard.
p. cm.
ISBN 10: 0-8109-5496-6 (hardcover)
ISBN 13: 978-0-8109-5496-0
1. Interior decoration—France—History—21st century.
2. Interior decoration—France—History—18th century—Influence
I. Trillard, Gilles. II. Title.

NK2049.A1L35 2006
745.0944′0905—dc22
2006016969

Printed and bound in Spain
10 9 8 7 6 5 4 3 2

harry n. abrams, inc.
a subsidiary of La Martinière Groupe

115 West 18th Street
New York, NY 10011
www.hnabooks.com